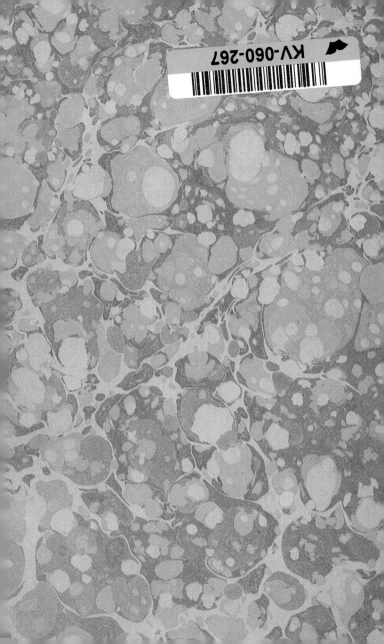

# THE ILLUSTRATED POETS

\*\*\*\*\*\*\*\*\*\*\*\*\*\*\*\*\*\*\*\*\*\*\*\*\*\*

Rudyard Kipling

# THE ILLUSTRATED POETS

# Rudyard Kipling

✳✳✳✳✳✳✳✳✳✳✳✳✳✳✳✳✳✳✳✳✳✳✳✳

Selected and with an introduction
by Geoffrey Moore

AURUM PRESS

First published 1992 by Aurum Press Limited,
10 Museum Street, London WC1A 1JS
Selection and introduction copyright © 1992 by Geoffrey Moore

A catalogue record for this book is available from
the British Library

ISBN 1 85410 202 8

1   3   5   7   9   10   8   6   4   2
1993   1995   1996   1994   1992

Picture research by Juliet Brightmore

Typeset by Computerset
Printed in Hong Kong by Imago

✳✳✳✳✳✳✳✳✳✳✳✳✳✳✳✳✳✳✳✳✳✳✳

# CONTENTS

| | |
|---|---|
| Introduction | 10 |
| Recessional | 13 |
| The White Man's Burden | 16 |
| The Female of the Species | 19 |
| Danny Deever | 24 |
| Tommy | 28 |
| Gunga Din | 32 |
| Mandalay | 37 |
| Gentlemen-Rankers | 41 |
| The Ladies | 45 |
| If — | 49 |
| Harp Song of the Dane Women | 52 |
| From JUST SO VERSES | |
|    How the Camel Got his Hump | 54 |
| 'Cities and Thrones and Powers' | 57 |
| The Beginnings | 58 |
| The Appeal | 60 |
| Notes | 61 |

✳✳✳✳✳✳✳✳✳✳✳✳✳✳✳✳✳✳✳✳✳✳✳

# INTRODUCTION

Rudyard Kipling was born in Bombay on 30 December 1865, the son of John Lockwood Kipling, a distinguished painter, sculptor and architect. His mother, Alice Macdonald, was one of four daughters who had married into the worlds of art and politics. Stanley Baldwin, the future Prime Minister, and the Edward Burne-Joneses were Kipling's cousins, ensuring that when the *succès fou* of Lahore came to London in his twenties he had an entrée into society.

But that was later. After an idyllic childhood in India he was sent at the age of five with his sister Trix to the English resort of Southsea. There, in what he called 'The House of Desolation', he was bullied and beaten by foster-parents. Holidays at the Burne-Jones's home in London were his only consolation. When he was twelve he entered the newly founded United Services College where, under the aegis of the headmaster, 'Uncle Crom' Price, he was considerably happier.

At the age of seventeen Kipling's father got him a job on the *Civil and Military Gazette* in Lahore. There he not only mixed with the Indian Civil Servants of the Punjab Club but with the squaddies and ordinary Indians he met in the town. His superb ear and profound interest in people gave him his copy, both in verse and prose. The verse, which often originated as column-fillers, was first published in book form as *Departmental Ditties* (1886), but it was *Plain Tales from the Hills* in 1888 which caught the public imagination. In that year, when he was twenty-three, Kipling went back to England to find that his fame had preceded him.

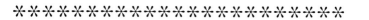

Through Andrew Lang he joined the Savile Club and wrote furiously. *Barrack-Room Ballads* and *Soldiers Three* further enhanced his reputation. In 1892 he married Caroline, the sister of Wolcott Balestier, an American with whom he had written a novel, *The Naulahka*, and who had died of typhoid a few months before. For a time the Kiplings settled in the Balestiers' home town of Brattleboro, Vermont. Two daughters, Josephine and Elsie, were born – the former, sadly, to die of pneumonia. To add to their tragedy, a son, John, was killed in the First World War. Kipling was not happy in Brattleboro and the family moved back to England, settling at 'Bateman's', a dark, Jacobean house at Burwash in Sussex. There he lived until his death in 1936 – of complications caused by undiagnosed duodenal ulcers.

Kipling's best-known 'soldier' poems – 'Gunga Din', 'Danny Deever', 'Mandalay' and 'Gentlemen-Rankers' – appeared in *Barrack-Room Ballads* (1892) and in *The Seven Seas* (1896) – from which I have taken 'The Ladies'. 'Recessional' was written on the occasion of Queen Victoria's Diamond Jubilee in 1897.

It is worth noting that apart from such inflammatory phrases as 'lesser breeds without the Law' (which referred to the Germans and not to what we now call 'the Third World'), the tone of 'Recessional' is the opposite of jingoistic. 'The White Man's Burden' – another poem of the 1890s – is a call to the United States to annex the Philippines, and thereby do them good. Kipling was quite sincere about this, having seen the devoted work that had been done in India by the incorruptible British middle-class.

If his work went out of fashion after the First World

War, the reason is not hard to find. Not only had public opinion turned against the concept of 'The White Man's Burden'; it was also embarrassed by the resounding truths which Kipling enshrined in 'If —'. With hindsight, however, we can see that he was not the insensitive bully-boy he is still sometimes taken to be. Far from being an imperialist exploiter, he felt it his duty to remind the British of the moral responsibilities of their role in the world.

For many years Kipling was unofficial Poet Laureate – although he refused the honour itself, as he also did a knighthood. He was prevailed upon, however, to accept the Nobel Prize for Literature in 1907. Like his friend George V, he was a modest and likeable man whose stories for children – particularly *The Jungle Book* (1894) and *Just So Stories* (1902) – are at least as well-loved and admired as his poems.

Kipling's ashes were laid in Poets' Corner in Westminster Abbey. It is a measure of his stature that he was admired not only by the general reading public but also by such eminent literary figures as Henry James and T.S. Eliot. His 'immense gift for using words, an amazing curiosity and power of observation, the mask of the entertainer and beyond that a queer gift of second sight' – all this, said Eliot, made him a writer whom it was 'quite impossible to belittle'.

He could have no finer epitaph.

GEOFFREY MOORE

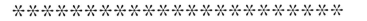

## Recessional
### 1897

God of our fathers, known of old,
    Lord of our far-flung battle-line,
Beneath whose awful Hand we hold
    Dominion over palm and pine –
Lord God of Hosts, be with us yet,
Lest we forget – lest we forget!

The tumult and the shouting dies;
    The Captains and the Kings depart:
Still stands thine ancient sacrifice,
    An humble and a contrite heart.
Lord God of Hosts, be with us yet,
Lest we forget – lest we forget!

Far-called, our navies melt away;
    On dune and headland sinks the fire:
Lo, all our pomp of yesterday
    Is one with Nineveh and Tyre!
Judge of the Nations, spare us yet,
Lest we forget – lest we forget!

If, drunk with sight of power, we loose
    Wild tongues that have not Thee in awe,
Such boastings as the Gentiles use,
    Or lesser breeds without the Law –
Lord God of Hosts, be with us yet,
Lest we forget – lest we forget!

For heathen heart that puts her trust
    In reeking tube and iron shard,
All valiant dust that builds on dust,
    And guarding, calls not Thee to guard,
For frantic boast, and foolish word –
Thy mercy on Thy People, Lord!

✳✳✳✳✳✳✳✳✳✳✳✳✳✳✳✳✳✳✳✳✳✳✳✳

# The White Man's Burden
### 1899
*(The United States and the Philippine Islands)*

Take up the White Man's burden –
  Send forth the best ye breed –
Go bind your sons to exile
  To serve your captives' need;
To wait in heavy harness
  On fluttered folk and wild –
Your new-caught, sullen peoples,
  Half devil and half child.

Take up the White Man's burden –
  In patience to abide,
To veil the threat of terror
  And check the show of pride;
By open speech and simple,
  An hundred times made plain,
To seek another's profit,
  And work another's gain.

Take up the White Man's burden –
  The savage wars of peace –
Fill full the mouth of Famine
  And bid the sickness cease;
And when your goal is nearest
  The end for others sought,
Watch Sloth and heathen Folly
  Bring all your hope to nought.

✳✳✳✳✳✳✳✳✳✳✳✳✳✳✳✳✳✳✳✳✳✳

Take up the White Man's burden –
    No tawdry rule of kings,
But toil of serf and sweeper –
    The tale of common things.
The ports ye shall not enter,
    The roads ye shall not tread,
Go make them with your living,
    And mark them with your dead!

Take up the White Man's burden –
    And reap his old reward:
The blame of those ye better,
    The hate of those ye guard –
The cry of hosts ye humour
    (Ah, slowly!) toward the light: –
'Why brought ye us from bondage,
    'Our loved Egyptian night?'

Take up the White Man's burden –
    Ye dare not stoop to less –
Nor call too loud on Freedom
    To cloak your weariness;
By all ye cry or whisper,
    By all ye leave or do,
The silent, sullen peoples,
    Shall weigh your Gods and you.

Take up the White Man's burden –
   Have done with childish days –
The lightly proffered laurel,
   The easy, ungrudged praise.
Comes now, to search your manhood
   Through all the thankless years,
Cold-edged with dear-bought wisdom,
   The judgment of your peers!

# The Female of the Species
## 1911

When the Himalayan peasant meets the he-bear
        in his pride,
He shouts to scare the monster, who will often
        turn aside.
But the she-bear thus accosted rends the peasant
        tooth and nail.
For the female of the species is more deadly than
        the male.

When Nag the basking cobra hears the careless
        foot of man,
He will sometimes wriggle sideways and avoid it if
        he can.
But his mate makes no such motion where she
        camps beside the trail.
For the female of the species is more deadly than
        the male.

When the early Jesuit fathers preached to Hurons
        and Choctaws,
They prayed to be delivered from the vengeance
        of the squaws,
'Twas the women, not the warriors, turned those
        stark enthusiasts pale.
For the female of the species is more deadly than
        the male.

Man's timid heart is bursting with the things he
must not say,
For the Woman that God gave him isn't his to
give away;
But when hunter meets with husband, each
confirms the other's tale –
The female of the species is more deadly than the
male.

Man, a bear in most relations – worm and savage
otherwise, –
Man propounds negotiations, Man accepts the
compromise.
Very rarely will he squarely push the logic of a fact
To its ultimate conclusion in unmitigated act.

Fear, or foolishness, impels him, ere he lay the
wicked low,
To concede some form of trial even to his fiercest
foe.
Mirth obscene diverts his anger – Doubt and Pity
oft perplex
Him in dealing with an issue – to the scandal of
The Sex!

But the Woman that God gave him, every fibre of
her frame
Proves her launched for one sole issue, armed and
engined for the same;

And to serve that single issue, lest the generations
     fail,
The female of the species must be deadlier than
     the male.

She who faces Death by torture for each life
     beneath her breast
May not deal in doubt or pity – must not swerve
     for fact or jest.
These be purely male diversions – not in these her
     honour dwells.
She the Other Law we live by, is that Law and
     nothing else.

She can bring no more to living than the powers
     that make her great
As the Mother of the Infant and the Mistress of
     the Mate.
And when Babe and Man are lacking and she
     strides unclaimed to claim
Her right as femme (and baron), her equipment is
     the same.

She is wedded to convictions – in default of
     grosser ties;
Her contentions are her children, Heaven help
     him who denies! –
He will meet no suave discussion, but the instant,
     white-hot, wild,

Wakened female of the species warring as for
    spouse and child.

Unprovoked and awful charges – even so the she-
    bear fights,
Speech that drips, corrodes, and poisons – even so
    the cobra bites,
Scientific vivisection of one nerve till it is raw
And the victim writhes in anguish – like the Jesuit
    with the squaw!

So it comes that Man, the coward, when he
    gathers to confer
With his fellow-braves in council, dare not leave a
    place for her
Where, at war with Life and Conscience, he
    uplifts his erring hands
To some God of Abstract Justice – which no
    woman understands.

And Man knows it! Knows, moreover, that the
    Woman that God gave him
Must command but may not govern – shall
    enthral but not enslave him.
And *She* knows, because She warns him, and Her
    instincts never fail,
That the Female of Her Species is more deadly
    than the Male.

# Danny Deever

'What are the bugles blowin' for?' said Files-on-
    Parade.
'To turn you out, to turn you out,' the Colour-
    Sergeant said.
'What makes you look so white, so white?' said
    Files-on-Parade.
'I'm dreadin' what I've got to watch,' the Colour-
    Sergeant said.
    For they're hangin' Danny Deever, you can hear
        the Dead March play,
    The Regiment's in 'ollow square – they're
        hangin' him to-day;
    They've taken of his buttons off an' cut his
        stripes away,
    An' they're hangin' Danny Deever in the
        mornin'.

'What makes the rear-rank breathe so 'ard?' said
    Files-on-Parade.
'It's bitter cold, it's bitter cold,' the Colour-
    Sergeant said.
'What makes that front-rank man fall down?' said
    Files-on-Parade.
'A touch o' sun, a touch o' sun,' the Colour-
    Sergeant said.

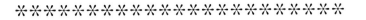

They are hangin' Danny Deever, they are
    marchin' of 'im round.
They 'ave 'alted Danny Deever by 'is coffin on
    the ground;
An' 'e'll swing in 'arf a minute for a sneakin'
    shootin' hound –
O they're hangin' Danny Deever in the
    mornin'!

' 'Is cot was right-'and cot to mine,' said Files-on-
    Parade.
' 'E's sleepin' out an' far to-night,' the Colour-
    Sergeant said.
'I've drunk 'is beer a score o' times,' said Files-on-
    Parade.
' 'E's drinkin' bitter beer alone,' the Colour-
    Sergeant said.
    They are hangin' Danny Deever, you must mark
        'im to 'is place,
    For 'e shot a comrade sleepin' – you must look
        'im in the face;
    Nine 'undred of 'is country an' the Regiment's
        disgrace,
    While they're hangin' Danny Deever in the
        mornin'.

'What's that so black agin the sun?' said Files-on-
       Parade.
'It's Danny fightin' 'ard for life,' the Colour-
       Sergeant said.
'What's that that whimpers over'ead?' said Files-
       on-Parade.
'It's Danny's soul that's passin' now,' the Colour-
       Sergeant said.
   For they're done with Danny Deever, you can
       'ear the quickstep play,
   The Regiment's in column, an' they're marchin'
       us away;
   Ho! the young recruits are shakin', an' they'll
       want their beer to-day,
   After hangin' Danny Deever in the mornin'!

# Tommy

I went into a public-'ouse to get a pint o' beer,
The publican 'e up an' sez, 'We serve no red-coats
    here.'
The girls be'ind the bar they laughed an' giggled
    fit to die,
I outs into the street again an' to myself sez I:
    O it's Tommy this, an' Tommy that, an'
        'Tommy, go away';
    But it's 'Thank you, Mister Atkins,' when the
        band begins to play –
    The band begins to play, my boys, the band
        begins to play,
    O it's 'Thank you, Mister Atkins,' when the
        band begins to play.

I went into a theatre as sober as could be,
They gave a drunk civilian room, but 'adn't none
    for me;
They sent me to the gallery or round the
    music-'alls,
But when it comes to fightin', Lord! they'll shove
    me in the stalls!
    For it's Tommy this, an' Tommy that, an'
        'Tommy, wait outside';
    But it's 'Special train for Atkins' when the
        trooper's on the tide –

✳✳✳✳✳✳✳✳✳✳✳✳✳✳✳✳✳✳✳✳✳

The troopship's on the tide, my boys, the
      troopship's on the tide,
O it's 'Special train for Atkins' when the
      trooper's on the tide.

Yes, makin' mock o' uniforms that guard you
      while you sleep
Is cheaper than them uniforms, an' they're
      starvation cheap;
An' hustlin' drunken soldiers when they're goin'
      large a bit
Is five times better business than paradin' in full
      kit.
    Then it's Tommy this, an' Tommy that, an'
        'Tommy, 'ow's yer soul?'
    But it's 'Thin red line of 'eroes' when the drums
        begin to roll –
    The drums begin to roll, my boys, the drums
        begin to roll,
    O it's 'Thin red line of 'eroes' when the drums
        begin to roll.

We aren't no thin red 'eroes, nor we aren't no
      blackguards too,
But single men in barricks, most remarkable like
      you;

An' if sometimes our conduck isn't all your fancy
      paints;
Why, single men in barricks don't grow into
      plaster saints;
  While it's Tommy this, an' Tommy that, an'
        'Tommy, fall be'ind,'
  But it's 'Please to walk in front, sir,' when
        there's trouble in the wind –
  There's trouble in the wind, my boys, there's
        trouble in the wind,
  O it's 'Please to walk in front, sir,' when there's
        trouble in the wind.

You talk o' better food for us, an' schools, an'
      fires, an' all:
We'll wait for extry rations if you treat us rational.
Don't mess about the cook-room slops, but prove
      it to our face
The Widow's Uniform is not the soldier-man's
      disgrace.
  For it's Tommy this, an' Tommy that, an'
        'Chuck him out, the brute!'
  But it's 'Saviour of 'is country' when the guns
        begin to shoot;
  An' it's Tommy this, an' Tommy that, an'
        anything you please;
  An' Tommy ain't a bloomin' fool – you bet that
        Tommy sees!

## Gunga Din

You may talk o' gin and beer
When you're quartered safe out 'ere,
An' you're sent to penny-fights an' Aldershot it;
But when it comes to slaughter
You will do your work on water,
An' you'll lick the bloomin' boots of 'im that's got it.
Now in Injia's sunny clime,
Where I used to spend my time
A-servin' of 'Er Majesty the Queen,
Of all them blackfaced crew
The finest man I knew
Was our regimental bhisti, Gunga Din.
      He was 'Din! Din! Din!
  'You limpin' lump o' brick-dust, Gunga Din!
     'Hi! Slippy *hitherao!*
     'Water, get it! *Panee lao,*[1]
  'You squidgy-nosed old idol, Gunga Din.'

The uniform 'e wore
Was nothin' much before,
An' rather less than 'arf o' that be'ind,
For a piece o' twisty rag
An' a goatskin water-bag
Was all the field-equipment 'e could find.

[1] Bring water swiftly

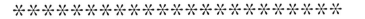

When the sweatin' troop-train lay
In a sidin' through the day,
Where the 'eat would make your bloomin'
      eyebrows crawl,
We shouted 'Harry By!'[2]
Till our throats were bricky-dry,
Then we wopped 'im 'cause 'e couldn't serve us all.
      It was 'Din! Din! Din!
  'You 'eathen, where the mischief 'ave you been?
     'You put some *juldee*[3] in it
     'Or I'll *marrow*[4] you this minute
  'If you don't fill up my helmet, Gunga Din!'

'E would dot an' carry one
Till the longest day was done;
An' 'e didn't seem to know the use o' fear.
If we charged or broke or cut,
You could bet your bloomin' nut,
'E'd be waitin' fifty paces right flank rear.
With 'is mussick[5] on 'is back,
'E would skip with our attack,
An' watch us till the bugles made 'Retire,'

[2] O brother    [3] Be quick
[4] Hit you    [5] Water-skin

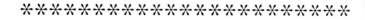

An' for all 'is dirty 'ide
'E was white, clear white, inside
When 'e went to tend the wounded under fire!
　　　　It was 'Din! Din! Din!'
　　With the bullets kickin' dust-spots on the
　　　　　　green.
　　　　　When the cartridges ran out,
　　　　　You could hear the front-ranks shout,
　　'Hi! ammunition-mules an' Gunga Din!'

I shan't forgit the night
When I dropped be'ind the fight
With a bullet where my belt-plate should 'a' been.
I was chokin' mad with thirst,
An' the man that spied me first
Was our good old grinnin', gruntin' Gunga Din.
'E lifted up my 'ead,
An' he plugged me where I bled,
An' 'e guv me 'arf-a-pint o' water green.
It was crawlin' and it stunk,
But of all the drinks I've drunk,
I'm gratefullest to one from Gunga Din.
　　　　It was 'Din! Din! Din!
　' 'Ere's a beggar with a bullet through 'is spleen;
　　　' 'E's chawin' up the ground,
　　　'An' 'e's kickin' all around:
　'For Gawd's sake git the water, Gunga Din!'

'E carried me away
To where a dooli lay,
An' a bullet come an' drilled the beggar clean.
'E put me safe inside
An' just before 'e died,
'I 'ope you liked your drink,' sez Gunga Din.
So I'll meet 'im later on
At the place where 'e is gone –
Where it's always double drill and no canteen.
'E'll be squattin' on the coals
Givin' drink to poor damned souls,
An' I'll get a swig in hell from Gunga Din!
        Yes, Din! Din! Din!
    You Lazarushian-leather Gunga Din!
        Though I've belted you and flayed you,
        By the livin' Gawd that made you,
    You're a better man than I am, Gunga Din!

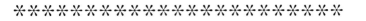

# Mandalay

By the old Moulmein Pagoda, lookin' lazy at the
    sea,
There's a Burma girl a-settin', and I know she
    thinks o' me;
For the wind is in the palm-trees, and the temple-
    bells they say:
'Come you back, you British soldier; come you
    back to Mandalay!'
      Come you back to Mandalay,
      Where the old Flotilla lay:
      Can't you 'ear their paddles chunkin' from
        Rangoon to Mandalay?
      On the road to Mandalay,
      Where the flyin'-fishes play,
      An' the dawn comes up like thunder outer
        China 'crost the Bay!

'Er petticoat was yaller an' 'er little cap was green,
An' 'er name was Supi-yaw-lat – jes' the same as
    Theebaw's Queen,
An' I seed her first a-smokin' of a whackin' white
    cheroot,
An' a-wastin' Christian kisses on an 'eathen idol's
    foot:
      Bloomin' idol made o' mud –
      Wot they called the Great Gawd Budd –

> Plucky lot she cared for idols when I kissed
>    'er where she stud!
> On the road to Mandalay . . .

When the mist was on the rice-fields an' the sun
   was droppin' slow,
She'd git 'er little banjo an' she'd sing '*Kulla-lo-lo!*'
With 'er arm upon my shoulder an' 'er cheek agin
   my cheek
We useter watch the steamers an' the *hathis* pilin'
   teak.
>    Elephints a-pilin' teak
>    In the sludgy, squdgy creek,
>    Where the silence 'ung that 'eavy you was
>       'arf afraid to speak!
>    On the road to Mandalay . . .

But that's all shove be'ind me – long ago an' fur
   away,
An' there ain't no 'buses runnin' from the Bank to
   Mandalay;
An' I'm learnin' 'ere in London what the ten-year
   soldier tells:
'If you've 'eard the East a-callin', you won't never
   'eed naught else.'
>    No! you won't 'eed nothin' else
>    But them spicy garlic smells,
>    An' the sunshine an' the palm-trees an' the
>       tinkly temple-bells
>    On the road to Mandalay . . .

✳✳✳✳✳✳✳✳✳✳✳✳✳✳✳✳✳✳✳✳✳✳✳

I am sick o' wastin' leather on these gritty pavin'-
    stones,
An' the blasted English drizzle wakes the fever in
    my bones;
Tho' I walks with fifty 'ousemaids outer Chelsea to
    the Strand,
An' they talks a lot o' lovin', but wot do they
    understand?
        Beefy face an' grubby 'and –
        Law! wot do they understand?
        I've a neater, sweeter maiden in a cleaner,
           greener land!
        On the road to Mandalay . . .

Ship me somewheres east of Suez, where the best
    is like the worst,
Where there aren't no Ten Commandments an' a
    man can raise a thirst;
For the temple-bells are callin', an' it's there that I
    would be –
By the old Moulmein Pagoda, looking lazy at the
    sea;
        On the road to Mandalay,
        Where the old Flotilla lay,
        With our sick beneath the awnings when
           we went to Mandalay!
        On the road to Mandalay,
        Where the flyin'-fishes play,
        An' the dawn comes up like thunder outer
           China 'crost the Bay!

# Gentlemen-Rankers

To the legion of the lost ones, to the cohort of the
     damned,
  To my brethren in their sorrow overseas,
Sings a gentleman of England cleanly bred,
     machinely crammed,
  And a trooper of the Empress, if you please.
Yes, a trooper of the forces who has run his own six
     horses,
  And faith he went the pace and went it blind,
And the world was more than kin while he held the
     ready tin,
  But to-day the Sergeant's something less than
      kind.
      We're poor little lambs who've lost our way,
        Baa! Baa! Baa!
      We're little black sheep who've gone astray,
        Baa – aa – aa!
      Gentlemen-rankers out on the spree
      Damned from here to Eternity,
      God ha' mercy on such as we,
        Baa! Yah! Bah!

Oh, it's sweet to sweat through stables, sweet to
     empty kitchen slops,
  And it's sweet to hear the tales the troopers tell,
To dance with blowzy housemaids at the regimental
     hops

And thrash the cad who says you waltz too well.
Yes, it makes you cock-a-hoop to be 'Rider' to your
      troop,
  And branded with a blasted worsted spur,
When you envy, O how keenly, one poor Tommy
      living cleanly
  Who blacks your boots and sometimes calls you
      'Sir'.

If the home we never write to, and the oaths we
      never keep,
  And all we know most distant and most dear,
Across the snoring barrack-room return to break our
      sleep,
  Can you blame us if we soak ourselves in beer?
When the drunken comrade mutters and the great
      guard-lantern gutters
  And the horror of our fall is written plain,
Every secret, self-revealing on the aching
      whitewashed ceiling,
  Do you wonder that we drug ourselves from pain?

We have done with Hope and Honour, we are lost to
      Love and Truth,
  We are dropping down the ladder rung by rung,
And the measure of our torment is the measure of
      our youth.
  God help us, for we knew the worst too young!

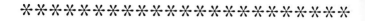

Our shame is clean repentance for the crime that
      brought the sentence,
  Our pride it is to know no spur of pride,
And the Curse of Reuben holds us till an alien turf
      enfolds us
  And we die, and none can tell Them where we
      died.
      We're poor little lambs who've lost our way,
        Baa! Baa! Baa!
      We're little black sheep who've gone astray,
        Baa – aa – aa!
      Gentlemen-rankers out on the spree,
      Damned from here to Eternity,
      God ha' mercy on such as we,
        Baa! Yah! Bah!

# The Ladies

I've taken my fun where I've found it;
   I've rogued an' I've ranged in my time;
I've 'ad my pickin' o' sweethearts,
   An' four o' the lot was prime.
One was an 'arf-caste widow,
   One was a woman at Prome,
One was the wife of a *jemadar-sais*[1]
   An' one is a girl at 'ome.

*Now I aren't no 'and with the ladies,*
   *For, takin' 'em all along,*
*You never can say till you've tried 'em,*
   *An' then you are like to be wrong.*
*There's times when you'll think that you mightn't,*
   *There's times when you'll know that you might;*
*But the things you will learn from the Yellow an' Brown,*
   *They'll 'elp you a lot with the White!*

I was a young un at 'Oogli,
   Shy as a girl to begin;
Aggie de Castrer she made me,
   An' Aggie was clever as sin;
Older than me, but my first un –
   More like a mother she were –

[1] Head-groom

Showed me the way to promotion an' pay,
   An' I learned about women from 'er!

Then I was ordered to Burma,
   Actin' in charge o' Bazar,
An' I got me a tiddy live 'eathen
   Through buyin' supplies off 'er pa.
Funny an' yellow an' faithful –
   Doll in a teacup she were –
But we lived on the square, like a true-married pair,
   An' I learned about women from 'er!

Then we was shifted to Neemuch
   (Or I might ha' been keepin' 'er now),
An' I took with a shiny she-devil,
   The wife of a nigger at Mhow;
'Taught me the gipsy-folks' *bolee*;[2]
   Kind o' volcano she were,
For she knifed me one night 'cause I wished she was
      white,
   And I learned about women from 'er!

Then I come 'ome in a trooper,
   'Long of a kid o' sixteen –
'Girl from a convent at Meerut,
   The straightest I ever 'ave seen.
Love at first sight was 'er trouble,

---

[2] Slang

*She* didn't know what it were;
An' I wouldn't do such, 'cause I liked 'er too much,
  But – I learned about women from 'er!

I've taken my fun where I've found it,
  An' now I must pay for my fun,
For the more you 'ave known o' the others
  The less will you settle to one;
An' the end of it's sittin' and thinkin',
  An' dreamin' Hell-fires to see;
So be warned by my lot (which I know you will not),
  An' learn about women from me!

*What did the Colonel's Lady think?*
  *Nobody never knew.*
*Somebody asked the Sergeant's Wife,*
  *An' she told 'em true!*
*When you get to a man in the case,*
  *They're like as a row of pins –*
*For the Colonel's Lady an' Judy O'Grady*
  *Are sisters under their skins!*

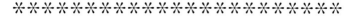

# If—
('Brother Square-Toes' – *Rewards and Fairies*)

If you can keep your head when all about you
    Are losing theirs and blaming it on you,
If you can trust yourself when all men doubt you,
    But make allowance for their doubting too;
If you can wait and not be tired by waiting,
    Or being lied about, don't deal in lies,
Or being hated, don't give way to hating,
    And yet don't look too good, nor talk too wise:

If you can dream – and not make dreams your
      master;
    If you can think – and not make thoughts your
      aim;
If you can meet with Triumph and Disaster
    And treat those two impostors just the same;
If you can bear to hear the truth you've spoken
    Twisted by knaves to make a trap for fools,
Or watch the things you gave your life to, broken,
    And stoop and build 'em up with worn-out
      tools:

If you can make one heap of all your winnings
    And risk it on one turn of pitch-and-toss,
And lose, and start again at your beginnings
    And never breathe a word about your loss;

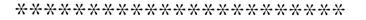

If you can force your heart and nerve and sinew
　To serve your turn long after they are gone,
And so hold on when there is nothing in you
　Except the Will which says to them: 'Hold on!'

If you can talk with crowds and keep your virtue,
　Or walk with Kings – nor lose the common
　　　　touch,
If neither foes nor loving friends can hurt you,
　If all men count with you, but none too much;
If you can fill the unforgiving minute
　With sixty seconds' worth of distance run,
Yours is the Earth and everything that's in it,
　And – which is more – you'll be a Man, my
　　　　son!

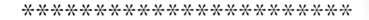

# Harp Song of the Dane Women

('The Knights of the Joyous Venture'
– *Puck of Pook's Hill*)

What is a woman that you forsake her,
And the hearth-fire and the home-acre,
To go with the old grey Widow-maker?

She has no house to lay a guest in –
But one chill bed for all to rest in,
That the pale suns and the stray bergs nest in.

She has no strong white arms to fold you,
But the ten-times-fingering weed to hold you –
Out on the rocks where the tide has rolled you.

Yet, when the signs of summer thicken,
And the ice breaks, and the birch-buds quicken,
Yearly you turn from our side, and sicken –

Sicken again for the shouts and the slaughters.
You steel away to the lapping waters,
And look at your ship in her winter-quarters.

You forget our mirth, and talk at the tables,
The kine in the shed and the horse in the stables –
To pitch her sides and go over her cables.

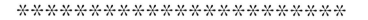

Then you drive out where the storm clouds
       swallow,
And the sound of your oar-blades, falling hollow,
Is all we have left through the months to follow.

Ah, what is Woman that you forsake her,
And the hearth-fire and the home-acre,
To go with the old grey Widow-maker?

## *From*
## JUST SO VERSES

# How the Camel Got his Hump

The Camel's hump is an ugly lump
   Which well you may see at the Zoo;
But uglier yet is the hump we get
   From having too little to do.

Kiddies and grown-ups too-oo-oo,
If we haven't enough to do-oo-oo,
      We get the hump –
      Cameelious hump –
The hump that is black and blue!

We climb out of bed with a frouzly head,
   And a snarly-yarly voice.
We shiver and scowl and we grunt and we growl
   At our bath and our boots and our toys;

And there ought to be a corner for me
(And I know there is one for you)
      When we get the hump –
      Cameelious hump –
The hump that is black and blue!

The cure for this ill is not to sit still,
   Or frowst with a book by the fire;
But to take a large hoe and a shovel also,
   And dig till you gently perspire;

And then you will find that the sun and the wind,
And the Djinn of the Garden too,
        Have lifted the hump –
        The horrible hump –
The hump that is black and blue!

I get it as well as you-oo-oo –
If I haven't enough to do-oo-oo!
        We all get hump –
        Cameelious hump –
Kiddies and grown-ups too!

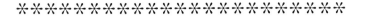

# 'Cities and Thrones and Powers'
## ('A Centurion of the Thirtieth'
### – *Puck of Pook's Hill*)

Cities and Thrones and Powers
    Stand in Time's eye,
Almost as long as flowers,
    Which daily die:
But, as new buds put forth
    To glad new men,
Out of the spent and unconsidered Earth
    The Cities rise again.

This season's Daffodil,
    She never hears
What change, what chance, what chill,
    Cut down last year's;
But with bold countenance,
    And knowledge small,
Esteems her seven days' continuance
    To be perpetual.

So Time that is o'er-kind
    To all that be,
Ordains us e'en as blind,
    As bold as she:
That in our very death,
    And burial sure,
Shadow to shadow, well persuaded, saith,
    'See how our works endure!'

\*\*\*\*\*\*\*\*\*\*\*\*\*\*\*\*\*\*\*\*\*\*\*\*\*

# The Beginnings
## 1914-18
('Mary Postgate' – A *Diversity of Creatures*)

It was not part of their blood,
  It came to them very late
With long arrears to make good,
  When the English began to hate.

They were not easily moved,
  They were icy-willing to wait
Till every count should be proved,
  Ere the English began to hate.

Their voices were even and low,
  Their eyes were level and straight.
There was neither sign nor show,
  When the English began to hate.

It was not preached to the crowd,
  It was not taught by the State.
No man spoke it aloud,
  When the English began to hate.

It was not suddenly bred,
  It will not swiftly abate,
Through the chill years ahead,
  When Time shall count from the date
  That the English began to hate.

# The Appeal

If I have given you delight
   By aught that I have done,
Let me lie quiet in that night
   Which shall be yours anon:

And for the little, little, span
   The dead are borne in mind,
Seek not to question other than
   The books I leave behind.

# NOTES ON THE PICTURES

p.6 *Rudyard Kipling, c. 1898*, pencil drawing by William Strang (1859–1921). National Portrait Gallery, London.

p.14 *Queen Victoria*, 1883, by Lady Julia Abercromby (1840–1915), after Heinrich von Angeli. National Portrait Gallery, London.

p.22 *Suffragettes being expelled after demonstrating at Westminster in 1906*. Photo: E. T. Archive, London.

p.26 *Coldstream Guards on Parade in Drill Order, c. 1910*, by Harry Payne (1858–1927). Reproduced by courtesy of the Director, National Army Museum, London.

p.31 *Wounded Guardsman, Crimea c. 1854* (detail), painted *c.* 1877 by Lady Butler (1850–1933). Reproduced by courtesy of the Director, National Army Museum, London.

p.35 *'Chedi', an Indian Water Carrier*, 1909, by Lady Burrard (1865/70–1928). Reproduced by courtesy of the Director, National Army Museum, London.

p.39 *Miss Hong Kong as a Burmese* by Sir Gerald Kelly (1879–1972). Photo: copyright © Christie's, London.

p.43 *Royal Horse Guards, Trooper in Stable Dress*, 1915, by unknown artist. Reproduced by courtesy of the Director, National Army Museum, London.

p.47 *Portsmouth Dockyard* (detail), 1877, by J. Tissot (1836–1902). Tate Gallery, London.

p.50 *The Lesson* (detail), by George B. O'Neill (1828–1917). Eaton Gallery, London. Photo: Fine Art Photographic Library, London.

p.54 *How the Camel Got his Hump*, 1902, illustration by Rudyard Kipling (1865–1936), from his *Just So Stories For Little Children*, published in 1902 by Macmillan and Co., London.

p.59 *Paths of Glory* (detail), 1917, by C. R. W. Nevinson (1899–1946). Imperial War Museum, London.

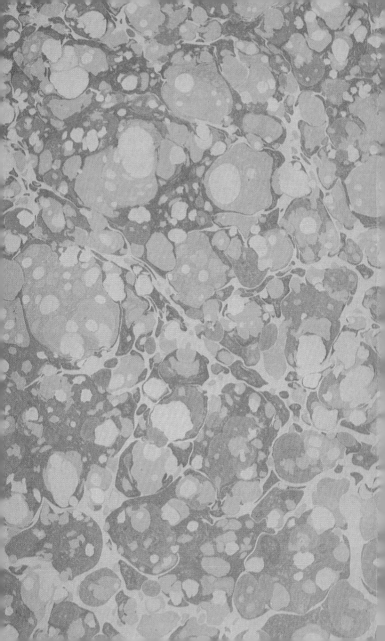